UNITED KINGDOM

By Theia Lake and
Gemma Greig

EXPLORING
WORLD
CULTURES

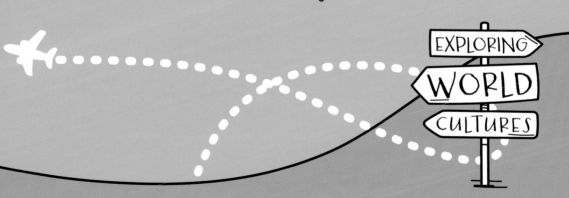

Cavendish
Square

Published in 2025 by Cavendish Square Publishing, LLC
2544 Clinton Street, Buffalo, NY 14224

Cataloging-in-Publication Data

Names: Lake, Theia. | Mattern, Joanne, 1963-.
Title: United Kingdom / Theia Lake and Joanne Mattern.
Description: Second edition. | Buffalo, NY : Cavendish Square Publishing, 2025. | Series: Exploring world cultures | Includes glossary and index.
Identifiers: ISBN 9781502670946 (pbk.) | ISBN 9781502670953 (library bound) | ISBN 9781502670960 (ebook)
Subjects: LCSH: Great Britain--Juvenile literature.
Classification: LCC DA27.5 L35 2025 | DDC 941--dc23

Writers: Gemma Greig; Theia Lake (second edition)
Editor: Theresa Emminizer
Copyeditor: Danielle Haynes
Designer: Andrea Davison-Bartolotta

The photographs in this book are used by permission and through the courtesy of: Cover, p. 8 Alexey Fedorenko/Shutterstock.com; p. 4 Gary Perkin/Shutterstock.com; p. 5 IR Stone/Shutterstock.com; p. 6 Peter Hermes Furian/Shutterstock.com; p. 7 Pandora Pictures/Shutterstock.com; p. 9 duchy/Shutterstock.com; p. 10 Michael Tubi/Shutterstock.com; p. 11 maziarz/Shutterstock.com; p. 12 Brendan Howard/Shutterstock.com; p. 13 William John Hunter/Shutterstock.com; p. 15 (top) matrobinsonphoto/Shutterstock.com; p. 15 (bottom) Espen Helland/Shutterstock.com; p. 16 James Kennedy NI/Shutterstock.com; p. 17 Gaid Kornsilapa/Shutterstock.com; p. 18 r.nagy/Shutterstock.com; p. 19 Vicky Jirayu/Shutterstock.com; p. 20 PhotoFires/Shutterstock.com; p. 21 Grzegorz_Pakula/Shutterstock.com; p. 22 13threephotography/Shutterstock.com; p. 23 INTREEGUE Photography/Shutterstock.com; p. 24 1000 Words/Shutterstock.com; p. 25 Steve Lovegrove/Shutterstock.com; p. 26 Richard Coomber/Shutterstock.com; p. 27 Ulmus Media/Shutterstock.com; p. 28 neil langan/Shutterstock.com; p. 29 BBA Photography/Shutterstock.com.

Some of the images in this book illustrate individuals who are models. The depictions do not imply actual situations or events.

CPSIA compliance information: Batch #CS25CSQ: For further information contact Cavendish Square Publishing LLC at 1-877-980-4450.

Printed in the United States of America

Find us on

CONTENTS

INTRODUCTION

The United Kingdom is a special place. It's a land of hills and lakes, stormy seas and island shores, stone castles, and ancient ruins. Part of what sets the United Kingdom apart from other places is that it's made up of four countries! The United Kingdom includes Wales, Scotland, England, and Northern Ireland. It's often simply called the UK. England is the most populous of the four UK countries.

There are many legends, or stories, tied into the UK's past. The legend of King Arthur is one of the best known.

4

Each country in the United Kingdom has its own capital city, soccer (called football) team, and parliament, or governing body. Each also has its own **traditions** and culture, or way of life. Traditional clothing, music, food, and even languages differ across the United Kingdom. Yet the rich cultural **heritage** of England, Wales, Scotland, and Northern Ireland is combined in this one United Kingdom.

The national flag of the UK is called the Union Jack.

GEOGRAPHY

The United Kingdom lies off the northwestern coast of the European continent, or landmass. Its only land border is with the Republic of Ireland. The sea surrounds it on all other sides. The English Channel, the North Sea, the Irish Sea, and the Atlantic Ocean all border the UK.

FACT!
The total size of the UK is 94,058 square miles (243,610 square kilometers).

This is a map of the United Kingdom. London is the capital city.

NORTH ATLANTIC OCEAN

NORTH SEA

Loch Ness
Aberdeen
SCOTLAND
Dundee
Perth
Glasgow   Edinburgh
East
Kilbride

UNITED
KINGDOM

NORTHERN
IRELAND
Belfast
Carlisle   Sunderland
Middlesbrough
Isle of
Man
Douglas
Blackpool   Bradford   York   Kingston upon Hull
Preston   Leeds
Bolton   Huddersfield
IRISH SEA   Liverpool   Manchester
IRELAND   Sheffield
DUBLIN   Stoke-   Derby
on-Trent   Nottingham
ENGLAND
Leicester
Wolverhampton   Coventry   Peterborough   Norwich
Birmingham   Northampton   Cambridge   Ipswich
Milton Keynes   Luton
WALES   Gloucester
Swansea   Newport   Swindon   LONDON   Southend-on-Sea
Cardiff   Bristol   Reading   Croydon
Bath   Dover
CELTIC SEA   Winchester
Southampton   Portsmouth   Hastings
Exeter   Poole   Brighton
Plymouth

ENGLISH CHANNEL   FRANCE

Guernsey
ST PETER
PORT
ST HELIER
Jersey

The River Thames flows through London.

At its widest point, the UK is only about 300 miles (500 kilometers) across. Great Britain and Ireland are the country's two main islands. There are also many smaller islands including the Hebrides, Shetland, Orkney, the Isle of Wight, and the Isles of Scilly.

A DIVERSE LAND

The UK is made up of very diverse, or different, lands. There are mountains, lowlands, hills, and rivers. The highest point in the UK is a mountain in Scotland called Ben Nevis. It is 4,413 feet (1,345 meters) high.

HISTORY

People first came to what's now the UK more than 2.5 million years ago. They formed groups called tribes. In 55 CE, a group called the Romans **invaded** the United Kingdom. They made huge changes, such as building roads.

Stonehenge is a prehistoric stone circle in Wiltshire, England. It was built between 3000 and 1520 BCE.

Later, a family called the Tudors ruled from 1485 to 1603. In 1603, the ruler, Queen Elizabeth I, died. She did not have a child to take over, so rule was passed on to Scottish cousins. They were called the Stuarts. Then, it went to the Hanovers. Later, the Windsors took power in 1910.

CASTLES AND RUINS

The United Kingdom's history can be seen all around the country. There are still many Roman ruins that can be visited today. There are also many castles, churches, and other historic buildings. Many of the UK's historic sites are protected, or kept safe, by law.

The Romans built Hadrian's Wall, pictured here. It can still be seen in Northumberland today.

9

GOVERNMENT

The Windsors are still the British royal family today. However, the royals (also called monarchs) don't have true power in the government.

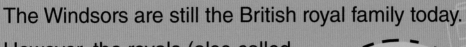

FACT!

England, Scotland, and Wales are often referred to as Great Britain, which is the name of the island they're on.

King Charles III and Queen Camilla were crowned on May 6, 2023.

The United Kingdom has a parliament. The head of Parliament is called the prime minister. Officials called members of Parliament help make laws for England and for the whole United Kingdom. Parliament in London makes big decisions that all parts of the UK must follow. Wales, Scotland, and Northern Ireland also have their own parliaments in their capital cities.

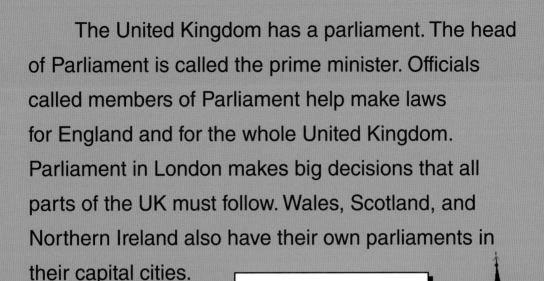

Parliament has two parts, or houses: the House of Lords and the House of Commons.

ACTS OF UNION

The United Kingdom was formed over time through the three Acts of Union. These were agreements that unified, or legally brought together, the four different nations. Wales was the first to join with England, then Scotland, and lastly Northern Ireland.

THE ECONOMY

Historically, the United Kingdom has had a very strong **economy.** The cities of Edinburgh, Scotland, and London, England, are two of the largest economic centers in Europe.

British currency, or money, is called pounds sterling.

A HISTORY OF MANUFACTURING

Before and during World War I (1914–1918) and World War II (1939–1945), many ships and planes were built in the UK. Cars and train parts are also made there. Trade with other countries is an important part of the economy.

In the past, the United Kingdom's most popular industry, or business, was manufacturing, or making goods. Agriculture (farming), banking, and oil production are big industries for the United Kingdom today. Tourism, or travel, is also a big part of the economy. London is one of the most visited cities in the world! The United Kingdom is thought of as a high-**income** country.

Sheep and cow farming are long-held traditions in the UK.

THE ENVIRONMENT

The United Kingdom is home to many special species, or kinds, of plants and animals. Forest animals include badgers, bats, foxes, squirrels, otters, and owls. Many important marine, or ocean, animals also live in the waters around the United Kingdom. Octopuses, sharks, seahorses, orca whales, and leatherback turtles make their home in nearby waters.

The UK is made up of forests and woodlands where large oak trees grow. There are also wet **marshes** called fens. Moors are open areas where heather and mosses grow.

NATIONAL PARKS

There are 15 national parks in the UK: 10 in England, 3 in Wales, and 2 in Scotland. People can visit the UK's national parks to hike, bike, boat, and watch wildlife. The Peak District became the UK's first national park in 1951.

The sun sets over North York Moors National Park.

FACT!

Peat moss is an important moss in the UK. It forms over hundreds of years in wet areas of land called bogs.

Red deer, such as the one pictured here, are the largest deer in Scotland.

15

THE PEOPLE TODAY

There are more than 67 million people living in the UK today. People living in the United Kingdom call themselves English, Scottish, Welsh, or Irish. Because the UK is made up of four different countries, its people bring together an interesting mix of traditions.

FACT!
London is the most **ethnically** diverse, or varied, area in England and Wales.

Although they're all part of one United Kingdom, each country in the UK has a unique culture and history.

Historically, England spread its **influence** widely across its **empire**, which went far beyond the United Kingdom. In turn, British culture was shaped by the many different people that Britain colonized. These cross-cultural influences can still be seen in the UK today.

Traditional clothing can be seen throughout the UK. Here, a man wears a traditional Scottish kilt, a type of wrap-around skirt, while playing a bagpipe.

CITY LIFE, COUNTRY LIFE

Historically, city life and country life in the UK were very different from each other. The UK is one of the most urbanized countries, meaning that most people live in cities. They may live in apartments called flats. Most country homes have a garden.

17

LIFESTYLE

Life in the UK differs greatly depending on where you live. Some people live and work in cities. Others are farmers. Some have jobs as businesspeople, teachers, or doctors. Others work in factories.

These double-decker buses say "Just Married" on them. Double-decker buses are a popular sight in London.

This traditional English country cottage, or small house, is in Cotswolds.

Today, many people wait until they are older to get married and have children. Many build their jobs first and have families later. The average age to get married in the UK is around 28 for a woman and 30 for a man. There are also many single-parent families. Most families have only one or two children.

EDUCATION

Children in the UK usually begin school around ages 5 to 7. Education is compulsory, or required, for children until age 16. There's a large push for higher education. Many universities in the UK are known worldwide for being very prestigious, or well respected.

RELIGION

Religious freedom is protected by law in the UK, so people follow many different religions, or belief systems.

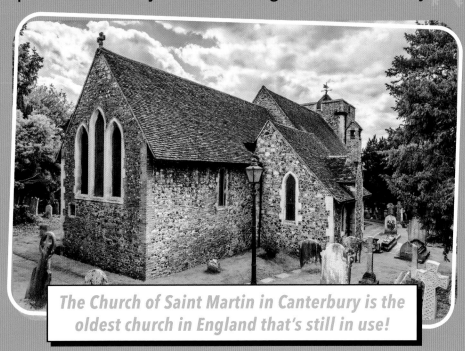

The Church of Saint Martin in Canterbury is the oldest church in England that's still in use!

OTHER RELIGIONS

Islam is the second-largest religion in the United Kingdom. About 5 percent of citizens practice Islam. Other religions include Hinduism, Sikhism, Judaism, and Buddhism. When people move to the UK from other countries, they often continue to practice their traditional religions in their new home.

Christianity is the largest religion in the UK. Although the UK does not have an official religion, historically it has been a Christian country. Today, there are two main branches of Christianity in the UK: Roman Catholic and Protestant. Most Christians in the UK are Protestant. Many belong to either the Church of England or the Church of Scotland. About 49 percent of UK citizens follow no religion at all.

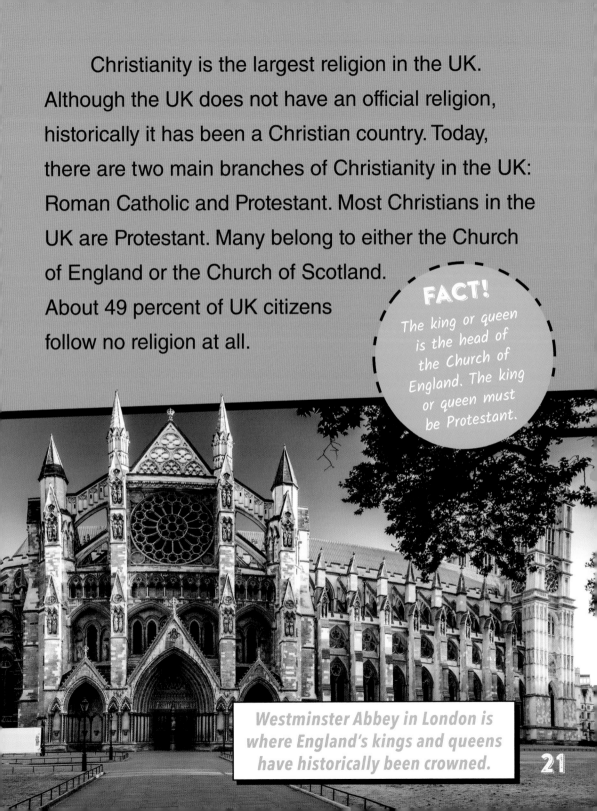

FACT!

The king or queen is the head of the Church of England. The king or queen must be Protestant.

Westminster Abbey in London is where England's kings and queens have historically been crowned.

LANGUAGE

English is the main language that's spoken in the United Kingdom, but it's not the only one! Welsh is spoken in Wales. Gaelic and Scots are spoken in Scotland. Irish and Ulster Scots are spoken in Northern Ireland, and Cornish is spoken in Cornwall, England. Many native languages are now taught in schools as a second language.

Many signs throughout the UK are written in both British English and a native language.

Fàilte do
dh'Eilean na Hearadh
Welcome to the Isle of Harris

There are many different English accents in the United Kingdom too. Somebody from London will have a different accent to someone from Newcastle or Glasgow.

LLANFAIRPWLLGWYNGYLLGOGERYCHWYRNDROBWLLLLANTYSILIOGOGOGOCH

Llan-vire-pooll-guin-gill-go-ger-u-queern-drob-ooll-llandus-ilio-gogo-goch

The Welsh town of Llanfairpwllgwyngyllgogerychwyrndrobwllllantysiliogogogoch has the longest name of any place in Europe! It's found on the Isle of Anglesey.

BRITISH AND AMERICAN ENGLISH

The English that's spoken in the UK is slightly different from American English. British English spells words differently than American English. Some words are different too. For example, a person in the United Kingdom would say "rubbish" instead of "trash."

23

ARTS AND FESTIVALS

The United Kingdom is the birthplace of many famous artists, writers, singers, and dancers. The love of arts, music, and theater can still be felt there today.

Different towns and cities have different festivals, or parties, and celebrations. Traditional Christian holidays are observed, such as Christmas and Easter.

Banksy is a famous street artist from the UK. His works, like the one pictured here at the Bristol Museum, can be seen throughout the country.

In the summer, many nonreligious festivals happen. Some are music festivals, dance festivals, or book festivals. The Edinburgh Fringe Festival in Scotland is held every August. It draws performers and theater companies from all over the world. The Glastonbury Festival in Somerset is the biggest festival in the UK.

MUSIC

Some of the biggest bands and musicians in the world came from the UK: The Beatles, Queen, Pink Floyd, the Rolling Stones, Led Zeppelin and many, many more. Britpop is a genre, or kind of music, that's based on **melodic** guitar music.

The Wales Millennium Centre in Cardiff Bay is a great place to see plays and shows.

FUN AND PLAY

Sports are very popular in the UK. Cricket is the national sport of England. Soccer, called football there, is the most popular sport. It is played by most children. Other common sports played in the United Kingdom are tennis, golf, and rugby. England, Scotland, Wales, and Northern Ireland each have their own football and rugby teams and will often play against each other in big tournaments, or series of games.

These children are playing cricket in Yorkshire, England.

Other fun activities include going to the cinema (movies), listening to music, and spending time with friends and family. Reading and gardening are also popular pastimes.

BAKING

Baking is another popular hobby, or pastime, in the UK. Many recipes are made specially to go with the British tradition of having afternoon tea. The British reality baking show *The Great British Bake Off* is widely viewed throughout the UK and beyond.

FACT!

Rowing is another traditional British sport. In rowing, teams race their boats by rowing with oars.

Fishing is another popular sport throughout the UK.

FOOD

The cuisine, or cooking, in the United Kingdom has been influenced by many different cultures. Curry is very popular there because of England's history with India, which used to be part of its empire.

Pork pies are very popular too. A pork pie is chopped pork meat and pastry with jelly separating the two. Black pudding is a kind of sausage. An English breakfast is a meal of eggs, sausage, bacon, grilled tomato, beans, and toast.

Fish and chips were the first takeout food in the United Kingdom, dating back to 1860.

Popular desserts include spotted dick, which is a traditional steamed pudding, and trifle, which is cake and berries with cream.

HAGGIS

Haggis is the national dish of Scotland. It's a meat dish made from boiled sheep's stomach! Inside the sheep stomach are minced, or chopped up, sheep's heart, liver, and lungs mixed with **suet** and oatmeal. Haggis is often served with turnips and potatoes, which Scottish people call neeps and tatties.

Cawl is a traditional Welsh stew made with lamb and vegetables.

GLOSSARY

artifact: Something made by humans in the past that still exists.

economy: The way in which goods and services are made, sold, and used in a country or area.

empire: A group of lands and peoples under one ruler.

ethnic: Of or relating to large groups of people who have the same cultural background and ways of life.

heritage: The traditions and beliefs that are part of the history of a group or nation.

income: Money made for doing a job.

influence: The effect something or someone has on the condition or development of something else.

invade: To enter a country to take control by military force.

marsh: A soft tract, or area, of wet land.

melodic: Having a melody, or pleasing rhythmic sounds.

prehistoric: Before written history.

suet: A type of animal fat.

tradition: A way of thinking, behaving, or doing something that's been used by people in a particular society for a long time.

FIND OUT MORE

Books

Mooney, Carla. *United Kingdom*. Minneapolis, MN: Essential Library, 2023.

Soundararajan, Chitra. *Let's Look at the United Kingdom*. North Mankato, MN: Capstone Press, 2020

Van, R. L. *United Kingdom*. Minneapolis, MN: Big Buddy Books, 2023

Websites

The British Museum
www.britishmuseum.org
Learn more about the history of the UK at the British Museum website.

***National Geographic Kids*: United Kingdom**
kids.nationalgeographic.com/geography/countries/article/united-kingdom
Learn more about the history, people, and environment of the United Kingdom.

Video

Tradfolk
tradfolk.co/music/songs/best-british-folk-songs/
Listen to traditional British folk music.

INDEX